Dolwyddelan Castle
Dolbadarn Castle
Castell y Bere

Richard Avent MA, FSA

D1493712

A History of the Castles

Introduction

Mounting guard over ancient routeways through the mountain fastness of Snowdonia, the castles of Dolbadarn, Dolwyddelan and Bere serve as lasting memorials to the castle-building achievements of Llywelyn ab Iorwerth, Llywelyn 'the Great', prince and undisputed ruler of Gwynedd from 1201 until his death in 1240. Llywelyn and his grandson, Llywelyn ap Gruffudd (d. 1282), were to dominate the politics of Wales for much of the thirteenth century. The strategic and symbolic significance of their strongholds was only finally eclipsed after the tragic demise of the house of Gwynedd at the hands of the greatest castle builder of them all, King Edward I (1272–1307).

Together, these three castles illustrate most of the design characteristics which are so distinctive of those few stone castles known to have been built by the Welsh princes. Reconstructing their history and attempting to understand their architectural development is not helped by the shortage of contemporary written sources. The descriptions in the tour sections of this guide are, therefore, drawn from a close study of the masonry of each castle and from comparison with other contemporary strongholds.

All three castles fell into the hands of the English Crown in the months following the death of Llywelyn ap Gruffudd in December 1282. Nothing further is heard of Bere after the Welsh uprising of 1294 and little of Dolbadarn after the opening years of the fourteenth century. Dolwyddelan, however, was to see a fleeting revival of its fortunes in the fifteenth century, when it was occupied by Maredudd ab Ieuan ap Robert. By the late eighteenth and early nineteenth centuries, both Dolwyddelan and Dolbadarn had become important subjects for landscape artists, particularly the latter which featured in one of the most celebrated paintings by J. M. W. Turner (1775–1851).

Later, in the middle of the nineteenth century, the principal tower at Dolwyddelan was restored in the current Romantic fashion, complete with fanciful medieval battlements. At the same time, the owner of Castell y Bere began to explore those castle ruins and discovered a range of artefacts including finely decorated sculptural fragments. Eventually, the ruins of all three castles were placed in State care during the 1930s and 1940s, after which they were cleared and consolidated for public display. They are now open to visitors and maintained by Cadw, the historic environment service of the Welsh Assembly Government.

The Princes of Gwynedd as Castle Builders

Despite constructing castles like Dolbadarn, Dolwyddelan and Bere, the Welsh did not readily adopt the Norman practice of building castles, preferring instead to live at their undefended *llysoedd* (courts). Out of more than 470 castles still

Part of a finely carved capital recovered from excavations at Castell y Bere during the middle of the nineteenth century. The quality of the stonework suggests that the castle was equipped to a high standard and demonstrates that Llywelyn ab Iorwerth (d. 1240) commanded sufficient resources to build on this scale.

Opposite: Castell y Bere, built on a rocky outcrop in the Dysynni valley, protected the southern flank of Gwynedd and controlled an important route from Tywyn, on the coast, across the mountains towards Dolgellau. Like the castles further north at Dolwyddelan and Dolbadarn, its design is typical of the stone-built fortifications raised by the Welsh princes.

Left: The princes of Gwynedd held power over most of native Wales for much of the thirteenth century. This mid-thirteenth-century manuscript illustration shows a Welsh prince as lawgiver and appears in a copy of the great Welsh law book of Hywel Dda (National Library of Wales, Peniarth Ms. 28, f. 1v).

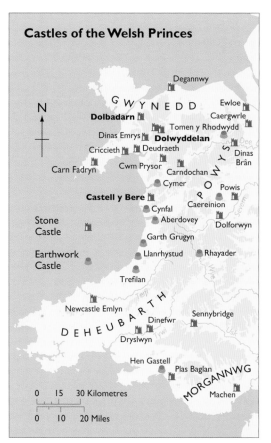

Castles of the Welsh Princes

Above: The Brut y Tywysogyon — *the* Chronicle of the Princes — *records the construction of a castle at Cymer in 1116. The earthwork remains are the earliest surviving castle to be built by the Welsh (National Library of Wales, Peniarth Ms. 20, f. 139).*

Below: Tomen y Rhodwydd, Denbighshire, built by the Welsh prince Owain Gwynedd (d. 1170) in 1149, is a fine example of a motte-and-bailey castle and equal to any raised by his English counterparts.

surviving within the modern borders of Wales, only seven per cent can be shown to have been built by the Welsh (although the original total must have been somewhat larger). The earliest reference to a Welsh lord planning to build a castle is found in an entry in the *Brut y Tywysogyon*, the *Chronicle of the Princes*. It records that, in 1111, Cadwgan ap Bleddyn was slain at Welshpool where he had 'thought to stay and to make a castle'. Five years later, we have the first recorded mention of a castle which has survived to the present day: the mound or motte at Cymer, near Dolgellau, erected by Uchdryd ab Edwin.

Throughout the remainder of the twelfth century, there are further very occasional references to the Welsh building castles. Where these can be identified today, they are of earthwork form, usually a motte either standing on its own or with an associated bailey. As such, they are indistinguishable from their English counterparts. Nowhere is this better exemplified than at Tomen y Rhodwydd in Denbighshire, which the *Brut y Tywysogyon* tells us was built by Owain Gwynedd (d. 1170) in 1149. Even allowing for the possibility that some of what we see today may be the result of restoration of the site by King John (1199–1216) in 1212, this is, by any standards, a superb example of a motte-and-bailey castle and would have been the pride of any Anglo-Norman lord.

Towards the end of the twelfth century we have the first references to Welsh-built stone castles. During his tour of Wales in 1188, with Archbishop Baldwin of Canterbury to gather recruits for the Third Crusade, Gerald of Wales (d. 1223) mentions two castles that had recently been erected in Gwynedd, at Deudraeth and Carn Madryn. If the present-day identification of these castles is correct, they are striking by the complete contrast in their location and style of construction. Deudraeth has been identified as Castell Aber Iâ, which now lies within Clough Williams Ellis's coastal Italianate village of Portmeirion, and consisted of a motte built up over a natural rock outcrop, originally surmounted by a stone tower. Carn Madryn is generally thought to be Carn Fadryn, the westernmost mountain on the Lleyn peninsula, which has a small enclosure of unmortared masonry on its summit within an earlier prehistoric hillfort.

The scarcity of known Welsh castles in the twelfth century has rendered impossible any attempt at establishing an overall pattern to their distribution. As far as we can see, they were not replacing the role of the *llys*, or court, as the centre of the Welsh administrative area, the *commote*. Neither do they appear to be linked to particular military campaigns, nor form part of a broader pattern of land control. Their most likely use was to control borders and routeways: for example, some of the castles built by Rhys ap Gruffudd (d. 1197) from the middle of the twelfth century onwards may well have been positioned to control the fluctuating border of his kingdom of Deheubarth in south-west Wales.

It was not until the thirteenth century that the Welsh began to build stone castles of a quality comparable to those raised by the Anglo-Norman Marcher lords. The finest examples are to be found in Deheubarth and Gwynedd in the north. Indeed, in Gwynedd, where Llywelyn ab Iorwerth rose to power at the beginning of the thirteenth century and was quick to adopt the stone castle, one might expect to see a more clearly defined pattern of the use of such strongholds by the Welsh. Building a castle was an expensive enterprise and a major drain on the finances of the princes. Construction would not have begun without a clear purpose in mind. One thing is immediately apparent, like their twelfth-century predecessors, with rare exceptions such as Degannwy in northern Gwynedd, these castles were not being built at the commotal *llys*.

The court of Gwynedd was itinerant, moving from one centre to another, and we know that castles came to feature in these itineraries. Their locations suggest that they were built primarily to serve a strategic function, as well as fulfilling a symbolic and political role. The princes were making it clear to Marcher lords, to other Welsh lords (many of whom owed allegiance to them), as well as to their own subjects, that they were the true masters of all they ruled. Neither can it be a coincidence that Welsh castles were sometimes used to house important political prisoners (p.15).

At various times the frontiers of Gwynedd extended right up to the English border. The castle built by Llywelyn ap Gruffudd at Ewloe lay close to the river Dee, and the one he began at Dolforwyn in 1273 lay almost within sight of the royal castle at Montgomery. Further west, Degannwy overlooked the coastal crossing of the Conwy, whilst castles at Carndochan and Bere guarded the southern border.

Above: The court of Gwynedd was itinerant and travelled between centres, including llysoedd (courts) and castles. This reconstruction drawing shows how the llys at Rhosyr, on Anglesey, may have looked in the mid-thirteenth century (Illustration by John Hodgson).

Left: At times, the border of Gwynedd lay close to England: the castle built by Llywelyn ap Gruffudd (d. 1282) at Dolforwyn, Powys, was just 4 miles (6.5km) from the royal stronghold at Montgomery.

Below: Cattle were important to the native Welsh economy and large ranches, or vaccaries, were located close to the castles at Dolwyddelan, Dolbadarn and Bere. This illustration appears in the Welsh law book of Hywel Dda (National Library of Wales, Peniarth Ms. 28, f. 23v).

Within the heartland of Snowdonia and on its southern flank, below Cadair Idris, the castles at Dolbadarn, Dolwyddelan and Bere controlled the principal routeways through the mountain massif. Their locations may have also been dictated by those of the princes' summer pastures or *hafotiroedd*. Important vaccaries, or cattle ranches, were located close to all three of these castles. In the immediate vicinity of Dolwyddelan there were no less than ten vaccaries capable of supporting 552 cattle all-year round. The castles would have provided permanent bases for the protection of this source of food. In time of war, mobile supplies on the hoof would have been crucially important to the survival of the men of Gwynedd if forced to retreat into their mountain stronghold.

Above: Llywelyn ab Iorwerth was the undisputed ruler of Gwynedd from 1201 until his death in 1240. This finely carved stone head was found amongst the ruins of his castle at Degannwy and may represent the prince himself (National Museum of Wales).

Above right: In 1205, Llywelyn gained further royal favour from King John (1199–1216) when he was granted the hand of the king's illegitimate daughter, Joan, in marriage. The princess was buried at Llanfaes Priory, Anglesey, founded by her husband, and when the house was suppressed in about 1538 the lid of her coffin (shown here) was moved to the parish church in Beaumaris.

The Rise of Llywelyn ab Iorwerth

Gruffudd ap Cynan (d. 1137), we are told by his biographer, 'delivered Gwynedd from castles' in 1094 by destroying the earthwork strongholds built earlier that decade by the Norman, Earl Hugh — the Fat — of Chester (d. 1101). The achievements made by Gruffudd, 'king of the kings of Wales', were indeed remarkable. His son, Owain Gwynedd, built on his father's successes, and by the time of his death in 1170, Gwynedd was pre-eminent amongst the native Welsh kingdoms. However, not for the first time, that primacy died with its leader as his inheritance was divided amongst his sons, according to Welsh custom.

Gwynedd was to be faced with thirty years of internal strife until, in the last years of the twelfth century, Llywelyn ab Iorwerth, a grandson of Owain Gwynedd, swept away the opposition of his uncles and cousins like 'the swirl of a great windstorm in a surly February', to emerge by 1201 as the clear ruler. His position was further strengthened that year by a treaty with King John, who recognized Llywelyn's title to all the land which he then ruled. Four years later, royal favour was further extended with the marriage of Llywelyn to Joan, the king's illegitimate daughter.

By 1210, Llywelyn had re-established the supremacy of Gwynedd over native Wales, but had also succeeded in incurring the wrath of the king. This was to manifest itself in a devastatingly successful military campaign by John in which he overran Gwynedd in a way that was not matched again until

Edward I's campaign of 1282–83. Only King John's political problems in England saved Llywelyn from total defeat in 1211–12. However, such a threat to the independence of Wales had evoked a degree of unity upon which Llywelyn was able to capitalize over the next few years. By 1218 he exercised total control over native Wales, and was to retain this position, despite minor setbacks, until his death in 1240.

Llywelyn recognized that if he was to maintain political stability, he needed to do more than just exercise control over his fellow Welshmen; he also had to have an influence on the affairs of the Anglo-Norman barons who controlled the Welsh March. To this end, he established a series of marriage alliances, marrying his daughters into the most influential Marcher families. The most important of these was that of Helen to John 'the Scot'. John was the nephew and heir of Ranulf 'de Blundeville' (d. 1232), the powerful earl of Chester who controlled land on the eastern border of Gwynedd. Almost as important was the marriage of his legitimate son and heir, Dafydd (d. 1246), to Isabella, the daughter of William de Braose, lord of Brecon, Builth and Abergavenny (d. 1230). As we shall see, these marriages were to have an effect on the design of Llywelyn's most sophisticated castles, those at Criccieth and Dolbadarn (pp. 11–12).

Left: King John was both a formidable ally and adversary. When Llywelyn incurred his wrath in 1210, the king launched a devastating military campaign on Gwynedd. This manuscript illustration shows the king hunting (British Library, Cotton Claudius Ms. D II, f. 116).

Below left: Llywelyn planned careful marriage alliances for his children to try to secure peace and stability in Wales and the March. The design of his later castles appears to reflect the influence of these powerful new allies, especially here, at Criccieth.

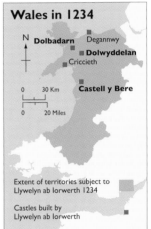

Wales in 1234

N

Dolbadarn   Degannwy

Dolwyddelan

Criccieth

0   30 Km

0   20 Miles

Castell y Bere

Extent of territories subject to Llywelyn ab Iorwerth 1234

Castles built by Llywelyn ab Iorwerth

The Dynasty of Gwynedd
Showing the marriage alliances of Llywelyn ab Iorwerth's children

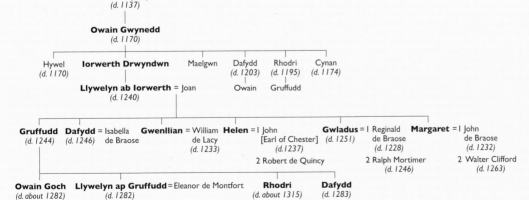

Gruffudd ap Cynan
(d. 1137)

Owain Gwynedd
(d. 1170)

| Hywel (d. 1170) | **Iorwerth Drwyndwn** | Maelgwn | Dafydd (d. 1203) | Rhodri (d. 1195) | Cynan (d. 1174) |
| | | | Owain | Gruffudd | |

Llywelyn ab Iorwerth = Joan
(d. 1240)

| **Gruffudd** (d. 1244) | **Dafydd** (d. 1246) = Isabella de Braose | **Gwenllian** = William de Lacy (d. 1233) | **Helen** = 1 John [Earl of Chester] (d. 1237) | | **Gwladus** = 1 Reginald de Braose (d. 1228) (d. 1251) | **Margaret** = 1 John de Braose (d. 1232) |
| | | | 2 Robert de Quincy | | 2 Ralph Mortimer (d. 1246) | 2 Walter Clifford (d. 1263) |

| **Owain Goch** (d. about 1282) | **Llywelyn ap Gruffudd** (d. 1282) = Eleanor de Montfort | **Rhodri** (d. about 1315) | **Dafydd** (d. 1283) |

A manuscript illustration of Llywelyn ab Iorwerth on his deathbed, attended by his sons Dafydd (d. 1246) and Gruffudd (d. 1244), from Matthew Paris's Chronica Majora *(Master and Fellows of Corpus Christi College, Cambridge, Ms. 16, f. 133).*

The great seal (cast), 1205–06, of Llywelyn ab Iorwerth (National Museum of Wales).

Llywelyn ab Iorwerth as a Castle Builder

The only reference we have to Llywelyn ab Iorwerth as a castle builder is an entry in the *Brut y Tywysogyon* for 1221 which informs us that he seized the *cantref* of Meirionnydd and the adjoining commote of Ardudwy from his son, Gruffudd (d. 1244), and that he 'began to build a castle in it'. This has generally been taken to be the stone-built stronghold of Castell y Bere, located on the south-western border of Gwynedd, in an area where Llywelyn sought to secure both overlordship of Meirionnydd and the protection of the southern periphery of his dominions. Political circumstances and architectural design have been the principal factors that have led to four other major castles being ascribed to Llywelyn — Dolwyddelan, Dolbadarn, Degannwy and Criccieth.

Three other castles have been considered as possible candidates. Near the southern border of Gwynedd, neither Castell Carndochan nor Castell Cwm Prysor are documented or have any distinctively datable architectural features but both could date to this period. At the very easternmost extension of the borders of Gwynedd lies Ewloe Castle, the dating of which has been the subject of much debate. In the absence of any convincing

evidence for an early date, it seems most likely that it was built by Llywelyn's grandson, Llywelyn ap Gruffudd, who is described in a document dated to 1311 as building a castle 'in the corner of a wood' at Ewloe in 1257.

As illustrated in a separate section in this guide, the castles built by the Welsh princes during the thirteenth century can be distinguished from their English counterparts by certain distinctive characteristics in their design (p. 13). Nowhere is this better illustrated than at Castell y Bere.

Apsidal Towers at Castell y Bere

It is generally accepted that most of the castle we see at Bere today was built from 1221 onwards by Llywelyn ab Iorwerth.

The main addition, consisting of thick walls linking the south tower and middle tower, is presumed to be English work dating from sometime after the capture of the castle by Edward I in 1283 (see plan on inside back cover). Other alterations, of uncertain date, include the construction of the courtyard buildings and changes to the entrance arrangements into the north tower and middle tower. There are, however, two puzzling aspects of the castle's overall plan, which may suggest that its development was somewhat more complex.

The south tower is of the characteristic Welsh apsidal — or elongated D-shaped — plan. In scale, it may be compared to examples of similar design at the Welsh castles of Ewloe and Carndochan, where they served as keeps. However, this tower is unusual in that it is both physically isolated from the main part of the castle, and has the fundamental weakness — not encountered in other free-standing Welsh towers — of a ground-floor entrance. Furthermore, it is overlooked by the rectangular middle tower which, standing on the highest point of the castle, must have functioned as the keep. All this may indicate that the south tower is a later addition, built either by Llywelyn or by his grandson, Llywelyn ap Gruffudd. If this is correct, today's middle tower would originally have been at the southern end of the castle with the outcropping rock sloping down to an external ditch — which is that now enclosed within the ditch yard. When the south tower was constructed, the sloping rock would have been cut away to form the platform now within the ditch yard. The reason for this alteration could have been to

Part of the north curtain wall of the castle at Degannwy, overlooking the Conwy estuary. Llywelyn had destroyed a castle here in 1212 when John invaded, but rebuilt the stronghold once the king had withdrawn.

provide further spacious accommodation at a time when defensive considerations may not have been so much to the fore.

The other distinctly unusual feature for a Welsh castle of the 1220s is to be found in the highly elaborate defended entrance with its ditches and two gate-towers, each with its own drawbridge and probably portcullis. This is precisely the sort of work upon which one might have expected Edward I to spend all or part of that sum identified in the building accounts for 1286–87 (about £207). Such a sophisticated entrance cannot be matched in any other Welsh castle. Indeed, even by the standards of English fortification, it would have been technologically advanced for the early 1220s.

It is, however, difficult to demonstrate that the barbican and gate-towers are a later addition to the original plan. In particular, there is no surviving structural evidence to suggest that the inner gate-tower was inserted into an earlier curtain wall. It is, of course, possible that its insertion may have

involved extensive rebuilding of the west curtain leaving no evidence of a junction between the old and new work. Alternatively, any evidence of such a junction may have been lost during modern consolidation of the castle masonry. All that can be said at present is that we must keep an open mind about the way Castell y Bere developed during the thirteenth century.

Above: In this aerial view of Castell y Bere, the two distinctive apsidal, or elongated D-shaped, towers can be seen flanking the northern (bottom) and southern (top) ends of the castle. Bere was almost certainly built by Llywelyn ab Iorwerth, but it may have been his grandson who erected the south tower.

Left: The apsidal tower at Ewloe Castle, Flintshire, most likely built by Llywelyn ap Gruffudd.

The Rectangular Tower at Dolwyddelan

Dolwyddelan Castle in Gwynedd is Llywelyn's traditional birthplace. However, it is very unlikely that the present structure would have been built in a Welsh context before 1170. Nor would the disunity of the last thirty years of the century have provided an appropriate opportunity for its construction (p. 6). The first work at the present castle, consisting of a keep of two storeys, must have been built by Llywelyn sometime between 1210 and 1240. This replaced an earlier castle — Tomen Castell — which occupied a rocky knoll in the valley bottom. At this earlier site, traces of a much less substantial sub-rectangular tower have been revealed by archaeological excavation.

In order to gain an idea of what Llywelyn's keep at Dolwyddelan might have looked like, we need, mentally, to strip away the nineteenth-century restoration of the tower with its false battlements. As originally constructed, the keep would have been the equivalent of almost a storey lower with a well-appointed principal chamber above an unlit basement. The pitched roof would have been set well below the battlement level. This was the typical arrangement adopted for all Welsh castle towers whether they were rectangular, apsidal or round. The only exceptions to adopt three floors were the round keeps at Dolbadarn in Gwynedd and possibly those at Dinefwr and Dryslwyn in Deheubarth in south-west Wales. While the rectangular tower at Dolwyddelan is the finest standing example, it may be no coincidence that Llywelyn's other rectangular towers at Bere and Criccieth are nearly identical in size.

The Round Tower at Dolbadarn

Dolbadarn Castle has the finest surviving example of a Welsh round tower. Where these towers served as keeps, such as here and at Dinefwr and Dryslwyn, the curtain wall abutted the tower. Elsewhere, less substantial round towers were incorporated into the line of a curtain wall, as at Bere and Ewloe, although not in the sense of an English mural tower forming part of an integrated defensive system.

The tower at Dolbadarn was consciously modelled on English examples. It was similar to structures erected during the first forty years of the thirteenth century by the lords of the southern March. As we have seen, Llywelyn had entered into

Above: A cutaway reconstruction of the keep at Dolwyddelan Castle as it may have appeared when first built by Llywelyn ab Iorwerth: the tower comprised a single well-appointed chamber set over a basement. The crenellations and curtain wall are shown without arrowslits, unlike the restored tower as it appears today (opposite) (Illustration by Chris Jones-Jenkins 1994).

Left: Dolbadarn Castle is dominated by a massive round tower, built by Llywelyn ab Iorwerth and consciously modelled on English examples in the southern March.

Above: William Marshal's round tower at Pembroke dates from the beginning of the thirteenth century and is believed to have inspired the construction of round towers found elsewhere in south Wales and the March.

Above right: The round tower at the Marcher castle of Bronllys, Powys, built by Walter Clifford (d. 1263) who was married to Llywelyn's daughter, Margaret.

Right: Ranulf 'de Blundeville's' twin-towered gatehouse at Beeston Castle, Cheshire, was probably the model for Llywelyn's gatehouse at Criccieth (English Heritage Photographic Library).

A reconstruction of Criccieth Castle as it may have appeared in about 1240. The gatehouse is similar to that at Beeston and the rectangular tower, to the left, is almost identical in size to that raised by Llywelyn at Dolwyddelan (Illustration by Ivan Lapper 1989).

marriage alliances with some of these Marcher families. He was clearly emulating the latest advances in military architecture, perhaps even employing English masons. Doubtless, he was conscious of his position as the premier Welsh prince and a major player on the wider political stage. He, too, merited a castle to match those raised at this time by his allies and adversaries.

Examples of English round towers can be found at Skenfrith, Longtown, Caldicot, Tretower and Bronllys (where Llywelyn's daughter, Margaret, was married to Walter Clifford, d. 1263). The inspiration for these towers is said to derive from William Marshal's great round keep at Pembroke Castle, built soon after he recovered Pembroke from the king in 1200–01.

Even by the standards of its day, Dolbadarn was a sophisticated structure with a portcullis at the entrance doorway and a particularly complicated newel stair: the spiral reversing direction halfway up. This compares favourably with the straight stairs found in the thickness of the walls of English towers. All of this is in contrast to the construction of an angular latrine projection, a fundamental point of weakness should the tower have come under attack and been subjected to attempts to undermine the walls.

At Criccieth Castle we can see another manifestation of Llywelyn's castle building being influenced by his English marriage alliances. There the gatehouse is probably modelled on that built by Ranulf 'de Blundeville' in the early 1220s at Beeston Castle, not far from the Welsh border in Cheshire.

The tower at Dolbadarn has clearly been inserted into a pre-existing castle of irregular plan, with two structures that are also generally referred to as towers, though they can never have stood to any great height. It seems probable that all the building work at Dolbadarn was Llywelyn's, with the first phase being built sometime in the second or third decades of the thirteenth century. The round tower, like the gatehouse at Criccieth, may well date to the last decade of Llywelyn's reign — the years after Dafydd's marriage to Isabella de Braose — and was followed by the reconstruction of the curtain wall. Either by then, or not long after, Dolbadarn had taken over from Llanbeblig (later Caernarfon) as the administrative centre of the commote of Is Gwyrfai. Labour services of the bondsmen of Llanbeblig were transferred to the lands around Dolbadarn.

Characteristics of Welsh Stone Castles

Between them, these three castles exhibit most of the characteristics that are so distinctive of the strongholds built in stone by the Welsh princes during the thirteenth century. Unlike their English counterparts, these castles tended to be of irregular plan, a pattern frequently dictated by the topography of their rocky sites. Natural defences were often supplemented by deep rock-cut ditches. Little account was taken of the need to provide flanking fire between towers and along the line of curtain walls. Towers were seen as distinctive strongpoints in their own right, with low curtain walls — generally of insubstantial construction — doing little more than defining an enclosure. Entrances consisted of simple openings through the curtain, often only accessible by foot or on horseback, and gatehouses were rare.

Welsh castle towers were usually of just two storeys with their pitched roofs set well down below battlement level. The unlit basement was often only accessible by ladder from the main apartment on the floor above. As in English castles of the day, towers could be round or rectangular. Alternatively, they might adopt the particularly Welsh 'apsidal' plan, consisting of an essentially rectangular tower, but with one half-rounded end. This apsidal, or elongated D-shaped, plan provided the convenience of a spacious rectangular living chamber, combined with the military advantages of a wide field of defensive fire power at the rounded end. At Castell y Bere, both the north and south towers adopt this distinctive plan in its most elongated form. In each case, the first floor clearly contained some of the best accommodation in the castle.

At the castles of Carndochan, near Bala, and Ewloe, close to the English border at Hawarden, similar D-shaped towers were employed as keeps. At the later Welsh castles of Dinas Brân, above Llangollen, and Dolforwyn, near Newtown, less extended towers were incorporated into the line of the curtain walls, with the rounded end projecting forward.

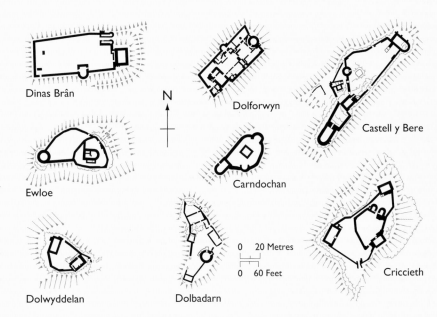

Dinas Brân

Dolforwyn

N

Ewloe

Carndochan

Castell y Bere

Dolwyddelan

Dolbadarn

0   20 Metres

0   60 Feet

Criccieth

Above: Comparative ground plans of castles of the Welsh princes.

Left: The D-shaped tower at Castell Dinas Brân was incorporated into the line of the curtain wall.

Below: Castell Carndochan from the air: the D-shaped tower that served as a keep can be seen to the right (RCAHMW).

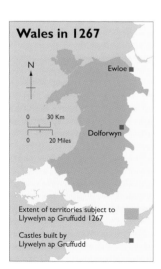

Above: The 1267 Treaty of Montgomery, under the terms of which King Henry III (1216–72) recognized Llywelyn ap Gruffudd's title as prince of Wales and his territorial gains (The National Archives: PRO, E 36/274, f. 327).

Right: An imaginative illustration of Llywelyn ap Gruffudd, prince of Wales, from a sixteenth-century manuscript (The Royal Library, Wriothesley Ms. quire B; The Royal Collection © 2010, Her Majesty Queen Elizabeth II).

Wales in 1267

N

| 0 | 30 Km |
| 0 | 20 Miles |

Ewloe ■

Dolforwyn ■

Extent of territories subject to Llywelyn ap Gruffudd 1267

Castles built by Llywelyn ap Gruffudd ■

Llywelyn ap Gruffudd

The years that followed the death of Llywelyn ab Iorwerth saw a major reversal in the fortunes of Gwynedd, culminating in the Treaty of Woodstock, concluded with King Henry III (1216–72) in 1247, a year after the death of Llywelyn's son and heir, Dafydd. Under the terms of the treaty, Gwynedd lost all its lands to the east of the river Conwy.

In 1255 Llywelyn's grandson, Llywelyn ap Gruffudd defeated his brothers, Owain (d. about 1282) and Dafydd (d. 1283), in battle at Bryn Derwin. Owain was imprisoned, and Llywelyn set about reasserting the authority of Gwynedd and thereafter extending its supremacy over much of the rest of Wales. In 1267 his position as overlord of the whole of Welsh Wales was recognized by Henry III in the Treaty of Montgomery when the English king accepted Llywelyn's homage as prince of Wales.

In the sixteenth century, at the time when the antiquary John Leland was writing, the traditional view was that Owain ap Gruffudd (also known as Owain Goch — Owain the Red) served his long captivity at Dolbadarn Castle. He was held there until 1277 when Llywelyn was forced to release him under the terms of the Treaty of Aberconwy (p. 16). In a contemporary poem, Hywel Foel ap Griffri laments Owain's captivity, describing him in the opening line as: '*Gŵr ysydd yn nhŵr yn hir westai*' ('A man who is in the tower, long a guest'). Hywel upbraids Llywelyn: 'Why does brother not forgive brother? It pertains only to God to dispossess a man'.

The reference to a tower in this poem suggests that Leland's sources may have been correct in identifying Dolbadarn as Owain's prison. A man of his status would, no doubt, have occupied the best chamber on the upper floor of the tower. He may, at times, have had the freedom of other parts of the stronghold, perhaps even being permitted occasional escorted excursions beyond the confines of the castle walls.

The dating of the second (west) tower at Dolwyddelan poses a problem as the surviving architectural detail is very limited. Clearly, it was built at a later date than the keep and curtain wall. The inclusion of a pre-existing ground-floor latrine on its northern face suggests that it replaced an earlier building, presumably contemporary with the

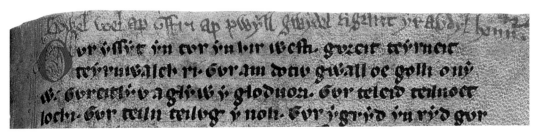

A poem by Hywel Foel ap Griffri, lamenting the captivity of Llywelyn ap Gruffudd's brother Owain (d. 1282). The sixteenth-century antiquary, John Leland, identified the round tower at Dolbadarn as Owain's prison (National Library of Wales, Hendregadredd Ms. f. 24a).

construction of the keep, and which was located next to the entrance to the castle. Very little dressed stonework survives in the later tower. The base of the jambs to the main doorway and the lower part of a narrow south-facing ground-floor window can be seen, but these can only be generally dated to the second half of the thirteenth or early fourteenth centuries. On the basis of this evidence alone, the tower could have been built either by Llywelyn ap Gruffudd sometime between 1255 and 1277, or by Edward I after he captured the castle in January 1283.

We know from his other building works, particularly at Criccieth and Dolforwyn castles, that Llywelyn was a builder of high-quality rectangular towers; therefore, the west tower at Dolwyddelan could be ascribed to him. However, a reference in a miscellaneous Wardrobe account of 1283 to expenditure by Edward I on the building of a new *camera* at Dolwyddelan Castle suggests an alternative, and perhaps more likely, occasion for the construction of this tower. We should note that the word *camera* is used loosely in contemporary accounts, not only for a large room or apartment, but also when referring to a whole residence or 'lodging'.

What we do know for certain is that Llywelyn's itinerant court would have stayed on occasions at Dolwyddelan and that he was here on 9 August 1275 when he sent a letter to the prior of Valle Crucis Abbey from the castle. Moreover, it was also at Dolwyddelan that Llywelyn appears to have kept at least part of his treasure.

Ten years after his recognition as the prince of Wales by Henry III, Llywelyn was to suffer a

Welsh Castles and Royal Prisoners

Imprisonment or exile was a not infrequent fate of those members of the royal house of Gwynedd who were seen as a threat to the authority of its ruler. Gruffudd ap Llywelyn (d. 1244), the illegitimate son of Llywelyn ab Iorwerth and Owain Goch's father, spent much of his life in prison.

Gruffudd was born sometime before Llywelyn's marriage to Princess Joan. The first historical reference to him is as one of the hostages his father had to hand over to John, following Llywelyn's defeat by the English king in 1211. Gruffudd was to remain a prisoner until 1215. Despite subsequently being granted land by his father, Gruffudd was to prove troublesome, and he was seen as a threat to his brother, Dafydd — Llywelyn's declared successor.

Llywelyn chose to imprison him in Degannwy Castle from 1228 until 1234.

In 1239, towards the end of their father's life, Dafydd confined both Gruffudd and his son, Owain Goch, in Criccieth Castle. In 1241, Dafydd suffered a humiliating defeat at the hands of King Henry III, and as one of the terms of the resulting settlement he was forced to hand over Gruffudd. The hapless prince was to spend his last three years at the Tower of London, where he fell to his death in an attempt to escape in 1244.

Criccieth is again referred to as a prison in 1259. One of Llywelyn ap Gruffudd's allies in south-west Wales, Maredudd ap Rhys Gryg (d. 1271), sided with the English in 1258, and was subsequently captured and brought to trial on 28 May 1259. Convicted of treason by his peers, he was imprisoned in Criccieth Castle until Christmas of that year. He was released upon forfeiture of land, having given his son as a pledge of future obedience.

Llywelyn ab Iorwerth's son, Gruffudd ap Llywelyn (d. 1244), spent much of his life in prison. This contemporary manuscript illustration by Matthew Paris records the prince's death when he fell attempting to escape from the Tower of London (British Library, Royal Ms. 14 C VII, f. 136).

The death of Llywelyn ap Gruffudd (below left), which took place at a skirmish near Builth Wells on 11 December 1282. His headstrong brother, Dafydd, was eventually captured: on 2 October 1283 (bottom), he was hanged, drawn and quartered at Shrewsbury (British Library, Cotton Nero Ms. D II, f. 182).

Below right: Siege engines, such as that seen in this manuscript illustration, were brought to Castell y Bere in the spring of 1283, and on 25 April the castle surrendered (British Library, Additional Ms. 10294, f. 81v).

humiliating defeat at the hands of the new king, Edward I, when he invaded Wales, having failed to receive the Welsh prince's homage. Under the ensuing Treaty of Aberconwy, Gwynedd was again reduced to its traditional heartland to the west of the river Conwy. But on 21 March 1282, Llywelyn's insubordinate brother, Dafydd, attacked Hawarden Castle and sparked off the war of 1282–83. Llywelyn was faced with an almost impossible dilemma. Torn between his fealty to the king and his loyalty to Dafydd and his people, Llywelyn was to side with his brother and led the Welsh resistance to the inevitable invasion by Edward. By the end of the year Llywelyn was dead, having been killed on 11 December in a brief engagement with English forces at Irfon Bridge, near Builth Wells.

In the third week of January 1283, Edward's army crossed the watershed from the Clwyd to the upper waters of the Conwy and, having secured Betws y Coed as a base, laid siege to Dolwyddelan Castle. The ease with which the constable of the castle, Tudur ap Gruffudd, surrendered suggests that he may have struck a deal with the English commanders even before they arrived at Dolwyddelan. By 18 January the castle was in English hands. Its capture, deep within the mountain fastness of Snowdonia, secured a crucial routeway near the watershed of valleys extending down to Conwy on the north coast, and to Harlech and Criccieth on the northern shores of Cardigan Bay. The castle was entrusted to a Welshman, Gruffudd ap Tudur, as constable, an appointment which a year later was confirmed for his lifetime.

Criccieth Castle, too, was soon in royal hands and the north coast secured westwards from Conwy to Caernarfon. In March, in the face of overwhelming forces, and with a rapidly dwindling band of followers, Dafydd, who had inherited Llywelyn's mantle, moved south to the vicinity of Castell y Bere. Edward's forces advanced on the castle from two directions. Robert l'Estrange marched west from Shrewsbury and William de Valence (d. 1296) moved north from Aberystwyth, coming together to besiege the castle with over 3,000 men, including the engineer, Master Bertram, whose siege engines had been used to good effect at Llywelyn's castle at Dolforwyn, Powys, in 1277. Although avoiding shutting himself up in the castle, Dafydd was unable to take any action to lift the siege. After holding out for ten days, Cynfrig ap Madog, the constable of the castle, and his garrison accepted an offer from the English of eighty silver pounds and surrendered the castle on 25 April.

Dafydd, meanwhile, fled back from Meirionnydd to Snowdonia, where he is to be found on 2 May somewhat futilely issuing two deeds from Llanberis, presumably from Dolbadarn Castle. Despite Edward's deployment of 7,000 troops in the hunt for Dafydd in May, it was not until 21 June that he was brought before the king at Rhuddlan having been taken 'by men of his own tongue'. He was subsequently to face a gruesome death at Shrewsbury on 2 October, when he was hanged, drawn and quartered.

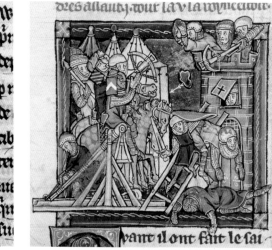

King Edward I

Edward was determined to consolidate his victory in Wales and following the 1276–77 war he had set about building new castles at Flint, Rhuddlan, Aberystwyth and Builth. In 1283, this programme intensified with the construction of new castles at Caernarfon, Conwy and Harlech and the repair and refurbishment of those Welsh castles that could usefully serve the political, military and economic needs of conquest.

The detailed financial accounts of Edward's building programme at Dolwyddelan have not survived, although some indication of the nature of his work at the site can be obtained from an account of miscellaneous Wardrobe expenditure during 1283. From this source, we know works were put in hand the very day the castle was taken. Directly the site was occupied, it seems the garrison was hastily equipped with camouflage clothing of white tunics and stockings, suitable for winter warfare in the mountains. The defences were to be reinforced with a siege engine made at Betws and carried down the pass to be installed at the castle. Ten stone 'cannon balls' of millstone grit are recorded in the accounts, and these may have provided the basic ammunition for this new engine. The principal building task, however, seems to have involved the raising of a new *camera*, which is probably a reference to the west tower.

Above: King Edward I was determined to subdue Wales following his victory in 1283. To this end he began a programme of building and repairing castles throughout native Wales, including Dolwyddelan and Bere. This late thirteenth-century manuscript illustration shows the king seated, holding a sword (British Library, Cotton Vitellius Ms. A XIII, f. 6v).

Left: An account of miscellaneous Wardrobe expenditure, which records various activities at Dolwyddelan including the construction of the camera (The National Archives: PRO, E 101/351/9).

Right: An early nineteenth-century engraving of Dolwyddelan Castle by David Cox (d. 1859), which shows that the upper part of the tower was not equipped with windows prior to the restoration of the keep in 1848–50. This suggests that Llywelyn's first-floor chamber was raised in height rather than a second floor inserted, most likely by King Edward I (National Library of Wales, Prints and Drawings, PZ 5940).

Below: A reconstruction of the rectangular tower at Dolforwyn Castle, following the English occupation of the site in 1277. A single high chamber was created by removing the intervening floor (Illustration by Chris Jones-Jenkins 2002, with modifications 2004).

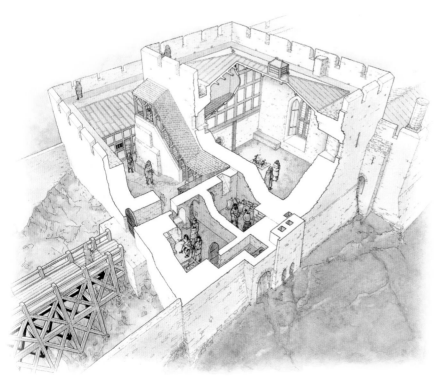

At some stage in its history, the earlier keep was heightened. In the absence of any distinctive and datable architectural features, two occasions might be suggested when this could have taken place. The first was after the castle's capture by Edward I, and the second — though less likely — was when it was reoccupied by Maredudd ab Ieuan ap Robert late in the fifteenth century (p. 21).

We know, for example, that Edward substantially rebuilt and heightened the south-west and south-east towers at the Welsh castle of Criccieth, and he may have adopted a similar approach at Dolwyddelan. The two-storey Welsh tower would certainly have been a somewhat squat structure by Edwardian standards. Edward may have been repairing a tower that had been damaged during the siege. If this were the case, it might have provided an opportunity both to heighten the tower and to introduce more spacious accommodation at the principal floor level. Indeed, a comparison can be made with the repair and modifications to Llywelyn's keep at Dolforwyn Castle following its capture by English forces after a short siege in 1277. Here, part of the two-storey keep was converted into a large single chamber rising the full height of the building.

In July 1283, work was taking place on a new bridge and a water mill at Dolwyddelan. A year later, in August and September 1284, £7 11s. 5½ d. was paid for repairs to the carpentry and leadwork of 'divers chambers' within the castle. The last reference to building works at Dolwyddelan appears in a letter, dated to sometime between May 1290 and October 1292, which records that Robert of Belvoir, who was chamberlain of north Wales, had paid for works, which are not specified, at Dolwyddelan as well as at the castles at Conwy, Caernarfon, Harlech, Criccieth and Bere.

Following the capture of Castell y Bere and the departure of the English army, five masons and five carpenters remained 'to carry out various works', the nature of which is unknown. We do know, however, that Walter of Huntercombe spent £47 13s. 4d. building a new 'chamber' whilst he was constable between March 1284 and October 1285. This may have been in preparation for one of the three visits made to the castle by Edward I during 1284. Shortly after the last of these, the king granted the new town of Bere free borough status. The decision to establish a town at Bere seems to be rather strange as there is no evidence of commercial or administrative activity here under the Welsh princes. Nor was the terrain particularly appropriate as demonstrated in 1284 by the need for seventeen woodsmen to cut a path for the queen's carriage between Bere and Tywyn. In the event, the town

was short lived and, although there were as many as sixteen taxpayers in 1292–93, it appears to have been abandoned by the end of the thirteenth century. The location of the town has never been identified with any certainty though it has been suggested that it lay on the flat plateau to the east of the castle.

A further £262 5s. 10d. was spent on additional unspecified construction at the castle between 1286 and 1290. Of this, almost £207 was expended between September 1286 and September 1287, perhaps on works associated with a general strengthening in response to the revolt led by Rhys ap Maredudd (d. 1292) in south-west Wales during June 1287.

In the autumn of 1294, with Welsh resentment of English government mounting, a much larger revolt erupted and spread over most of the country. In the north, under the leadership of Madog ap Llywelyn, the Welsh overran the castle and town of Caernarfon and slew the sheriff. By 18 October the king was issuing orders to Richard Fitzalan, earl of Arundel, to ensure that Bere was adequately supplied and that everything was being done to secure the safety of the castle and its garrison. On 27 October, he sent further instructions to the earl and others to prepare to mount an expedition to relieve the castle — 'whose safety we desire with all our heart' — presumably by now under siege. Robert Fitzwalter, its constable, had been hastily recalled from an expedition at Portsmouth

An artist's impression of how Castell y Bere may have looked towards the end of the thirteenth century, following the English capture of the castle in 1283 and the construction of the ditch yard walls. The upper levels of the towers are conjectural, based on evidence from other Welsh stone-built castles (Illustration by Chris Jones-Jenkins 2004).

Above: There is no record of Edward I undertaking building work at Dolbadarn Castle. Although it served as the centre of a royal manor in the early years of the fourteenth century, its later history is obscure and it next appears as ruinous in eighteenth-century topographical engravings. This detail of the round tower is taken from a 1742 engraving of the castle by Samuel and Nathaniel Buck.

and was to join the relieving force. His absence may well have encouraged the rebels to besiege the castle in the first place. After this the records are silent. The castle may or may not have been relieved. The only clue to its fate lies in archaeological evidence from work at the site in the middle of the nineteenth century and during the 1950s and 1960s. This showed that some of the buildings in the courtyard and the well house had been destroyed by burning, and that occupation at the castle had ceased sometime towards the end of the thirteenth century.

There is no record of Edward undertaking any work at Dolbadarn. This is hardly surprising, as the

Right: In 1488, Maredudd ab Ieuan ap Robert purchased the lease of Dolwyddelan Castle and took up residence with his family. This illustration of Maredudd is taken from a brass that survives in the church at Dolwyddelan.

castle's strategic value ended with the construction of Edward's magnificent new fortress at Caernarfon. Indeed, the only reference in the Edwardian accounts is to the removal of timbers from Dolbadarn to Caernarfon in 1284. These may have come from the hall, either its roof timbers, or possibly the timber frame which may have rested on the surviving stone footings. We know, for example, that Edward had the Welsh timber halls at Conwy, Aberffraw and Ystumgwern carefully dismantled and re-erected in the wards of his new castles at Caernarfon and Harlech. Although the reuse of building timbers is not unusual in the Middle Ages, in the context of Edward's massive programme of building works, these actions must also be seen as having a strong symbolic significance. The hall, which lay at the very core of Welsh princely society, was being physically brought within the compass of Edward's new castles.

Despite this partial dismantling, Dolbadarn continued in use as the centre of a royal manor, and houses within the castle were being repaired by the sheriff of Caernarfon in 1303–04. The east building, cutting across the line of the Welsh curtain wall, is clearly a later addition and must date to this period.

The Fifteenth Century

In 1488 Maredudd ab Ieuan ap Robert, the great-grandfather of Sir John Wynn (biographer of the Gwydir family and our source of information on Maredudd), purchased the lease of Dolwyddelan from the executors of Sir Ralph Birkenhead, formerly chamberlain of north Wales. Maredudd and his wife, Alice, together with their two daughters, moved into a castle which was described as being 'in part thereof habitable' having been the place where one Hywel ab Ieuan ap Rhys 'captain of the country, an outlaw' had dwelt some years before.

Maredudd's reasons for moving from his previous house, just to the east of Caernarfon, appear to have been to find a larger home for his expanding family and to return to 'his inheritance in Eifionydd'. What he found was a countryside that was unruly and without any form of law and order. Even some years later, when he had built himself a new house at Penamnen and a new church in Dolwyddelan, both about a mile (1.6km) from the castle and one

A superb watercolour of Dolwyddelan Castle, with Snowdon beyond, by Peter de Wint (d. 1849). The painting provides valuable clues about the condition of the castle before it was restored between 1848 and 1850 (National Library of Wales, Prints and Drawings, PB 3279).

another, it was said, 'that he dared not to go out to church on a Sunday from his house at Penamnen but that he must leave the same guarded with men and have the doors sure barred and bolted and a watchman to stand guard at Y Garreg Big during divine service (being a rock whence he might see both the church and the house and raise the cry if the house were assaulted)'.

In such circumstances it is hardly surprising that Maredudd chose a castle as his first home in the area, and he must have taken on at least its partial rehabilitation. It is unlikely that the keep alone would have adequately served the needs of his family and he may have preferred the west tower for his main accommodation, with its spacious chambers at both ground- and first-floor levels. He may have adapted the keep to his needs but, as mentioned above (p. 18), it seems unlikely that he would have gone to the trouble of heightening it. Maredudd's need for security against the more untrustworthy element amongst his fellow countrymen may have resulted in repairs to the curtain wall. In addition, the straight stair leading up to the wall-walk at the southern end of the west tower may also be his work.

Later History

By the middle of the eighteenth century, when the castles at Dolbadarn and Dolwyddelan feature in the topographical engravings of Samuel and Nathaniel Buck, both strongholds were ruinous. In their romantic and picturesque settings, and with the mountains of Snowdonia as a dramatic backdrop, they became popular subjects, particularly Dolbadarn, for travellers and artists (p. 22). Travel had become difficult in much of Europe because of the political turmoil the Continent was going through in the late eighteenth and early nineteenth centuries. Some of the more detailed and accurate representations of Dolwyddelan made at this time provide a valuable record of the condition of the castle before it underwent a major programme of restoration at the hands of Lord Willoughby de Eresby in 1848–50.

All three castles were eventually placed in the guardianship of the State: Dolwyddelan by Mrs C. Williams of Bryn Tirion in 1930, Dolbadarn by Sir Michael Duff of the Vaynol Estate in 1941 and Castell y Bere by Lt. Col. Charles Edward Corbett in 1949.

An early photograph of Dolwyddelan Castle, taken not long after the 1848–50 restoration work. The new masonry in the northern end wall of the keep is particularly clear (Crown copyright: National Monuments Record for Wales).

Dolbadarn: Sublime and Picturesque

Landscape became one of the most important aspects of British art from the middle of the eighteenth century onwards. Wales, particularly the rugged mountains of Snowdonia, was to play a major role in this new cultural movement. Interest in Welsh scenery grew steadily from 1760. By 1800, the summer exhibition at the Royal Academy included thirty pictures of Wales alone.

Of all the scenes in Wales, that of the ruined round tower of Dolbadarn Castle, set against the magnificent backdrop of Snowdon, the twin lakes of Padarn and Peris, the distant pass and an ever-changing sky, evoked the greatest curiosity and interest. These natural features were further enhanced by the history and legend which surrounded Owain Goch's long captivity, that great injustice of brother towards brother.

The typical composition almost invariably shows the castle in the middle ground, with mountains behind and lake to the fore, often with figures placed into an otherwise wild landscape. It is just such a scene which serves to reflect and exemplify the two important aesthetic notions which became popular at this time: the Sublime and the Picturesque.

Between 1756 and 1763, Edmund Burke in three crucial aesthetic texts propounded his view of the Sublime. Beauty might be small, smooth and polished within a great rugged, neglected landscape. 'All general privations are great, because they are terrible: Vacuity, Darkness, Solitude and Silence'. Dolbadarn Castle has these qualities. It stands alone, a gloomy isolated tower, windswept within a stark mountain landscape, characterized by a foreboding silence and solitude. This image is captured to perfection in Turner's famous picture of the castle exhibited at the Royal Academy in 1800.

The Reverend William Gilpin, the apostle of the Picturesque, stressed the use of simple rules. A reliance on traditional art objects, and the right of the individual to alter nature to conform to pictures. The artist needed to supply composition to the raw materials of nature in order to produce a harmonious design. A.V. Copley Fielding's view of Dolbadarn, with the tiny tower in the centre of the picture, framed by mountain and water, is a fine example of the pure Picturesque.

Right: A. V. Copley Fielding (d. 1855) painted this watercolour of Dolbadarn in about 1810. With the tiny tower in the centre of the picture, framed by mountain and water, it is a fine example of the Picturesque notion of landscape painting (National Library of Wales, Prints and Drawings, PD 5720).

Opposite: J. M. W. Turner (d. 1851) presented this magnificent painting of Dolbadarn to the Royal Academy as his Diploma work on being elected RA in 1802. The picture captures the notion of the Sublime perfectly with the gloomy isolated tower standing in a stark mountain landscape (Royal Academy of Arts, London).

A Tour of Dolwyddelan Castle

Dolwyddelan Castle overlooks the Lledr valley, and stands on a rocky knoll forming part of a ridge on the southern slopes of Moel Siabod. The medieval road, which led up from the Vale of Conwy into Meirionnydd, ran not in the valley, but along the higher ground, passing close to the west tower of the castle.

Today, you approach the site along a rough track from the north-east. This, and the opposite side of the castle, were protected by rock-cut ditches, with low outer banks, which cut across the ridge. Natural defences were provided to the north by an area of marshy land and to the south by a precipitous drop down into the valley.

A short flight of steps over a modern causeway now crosses the northern end of the eastern ditch. The original arrangement probably involved a timber bridge leading to a plain entrance through the curtain wall into the courtyard. Once in the courtyard, the impressive rectangular stone keep dominates the site and is its principal attraction. As originally built by Llywelyn ab Iorwerth in the early thirteenth century, this was of just two storeys like the ruins of the second tower built later in the century, probably by Edward I (pp. 14–15, 17, 28). Initially freestanding, Llywelyn soon enclosed the keep with a stone curtain wall. The tower itself was raised in height, again most likely by Edward I after the castle had fallen to the English in 1283. However, there is no indication that another floor was inserted and, instead, the principal chamber may have extended to the full height of the building. Maredudd ab Ieuan ap Robert may have made further alterations in the fifteenth century but if so, these are not readily apparent. The final alterations were made between 1848 and 1850 by Lord Willoughby de Eresby (p. 21).

To the left of the keep, in the south-east corner of the courtyard, there is another opening in the curtain, and by looking over the wall in the corner you can see a further length of curtain with a postern doorway leading out of the castle. This small area appears to have been enclosed sometime after the keep and main curtain wall were built, perhaps at the same time as the castle was strengthened with the addition of the west tower, towards the end of the thirteenth century. The only means of gaining access to this area would have been by stairs leading down from the main curtain, or by a ladder.

The Keep

Exterior

We know from what appears to be an accurate drawing, dating to 1815, that the upper part of the courtyard-facing side, together with much of the southern end of the keep, was ruined by the early nineteenth century. Two other illustrations, dating from approximately the same period, show that a V-shaped area of masonry was also missing from the upper half of the northern end of the tower. All of this was repaired and restored by Lord Willoughby de Eresby between 1848 and 1850.

Opposite: Dolwyddelan Castle is set on a rocky knoll overlooking the Lledr valley, where the modern road now runs. The medieval road, however, ran close to the smaller west tower, seen in the foreground of this picture.

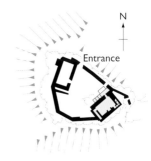

Two illustrations showing the castle before restoration in 1848–50. That to the left shows the ruinous state of the courtyard-facing wall in 1815. The right-hand sketch, by Sir Richard Colt Hoare (d. 1838), shows the V-shaped area of masonry missing from the northern keep wall.

Above: A reconstruction of Dolwyddelan Castle as it may have looked in the later thirteenth century. The crenellations on both towers and the curtain wall are shown equipped with arrowslits (Illustration by Chris Jones-Jenkins 1994).

The courtyard facing wall and southern end of the keep, including the latrine projection, were heavily restored in 1848–50. The projecting mock slab drains and battlements are entirely fanciful.

If you look at the outside of the keep, one of the first things that you notice is that the masonry above the horizontal row of projecting mock slab drains, along with much of the southern wall, and including the latrine projection, consists of regularly-laid slabs of the local shale. This characterizes the nineteenth-century work and is in marked contrast to the more mixed nature of the stone below, some of which is obscured by rendering.

The first-floor window, to the right of the entrance to the keep, is in its original medieval position, although its surround appears to have been renewed in the nineteenth century. The two other first-floor windows on the opposite side of the tower are also medieval. None of the second-floor windows appears in any of the early illustrations, and all three seem to have been introduced as part of the nineteenth-century work.

At the top of the flight of stone steps leading to the entrance, in the wall of the keep, you can see one side of the original doorway that led into a fore-building, with a slot for a drawbar to secure the door. Although now ruinous, the fore-building would have protected the present doorway into the keep and had the added sophistication of a pit for a wooden drawbridge which, in time of emergency, might have been removed or raised against the door.

Interior

Once inside the tower, you find yourself in a large room open to the roof. The impression, however, is deceptive for, as we have seen, the present arrangements are largely the result of the heightening of the keep and the nineteenth-century restoration.

As originally built in the early thirteenth century by Llywelyn ab Iorwerth, the room in which you now stand would have been about half the height and would have served as the principal chamber of the tower. It was situated over a basement, which could be entered through a trapdoor in the floor and was lit by three small openings in the outer wall.

The longer side walls of this period mostly survive at first-floor level, including the offset to support the roof timbers, together with the inner face of the southern end wall, in which the line of the original steeply pitched roof gable can still be seen. The walls of Llywelyn's keep would have risen above this gable level to the original battlements. Although lower than the present battlements, the initial arrangement would have enclosed and protected the keep roof (see reconstruction drawing, p.11). Very little of the original masonry appears to have survived in the northern end wall, which was substantially rebuilt during the nineteenth-century restoration. Consequently there is no evidence of the roof gable in this wall to match that at the opposite end of the tower.

At this first-floor level, the apartment is lit by two windows in the outer wall and one in the wall facing the courtyard. All have wide embrasures with seats. The window to the left of the fireplace has had a doorway inserted through the side of the embrasure, and this provides access to the straight stair leading to the roof. The fireplace in the middle of the wall is a nineteenth-century reconstruction, although its back is of earlier date. A doorway in the western corner of the room may be a nineteenth-century replacement for an earlier medieval door leading to a passage that extends down in the thickness of the wall to a latrine chamber in the southern corner of the tower.

The original form of the upper part of the floor, once the tower had been heightened, probably by Edward I in the later thirteenth century, remains somewhat uncertain, though the joist holes just below the present roof probably indicate the height of the ceiling at this time. There is no evidence of a second-floor entrance from the stairs contained within the wall thickness, though the inner face of this wall may have been substantially rebuilt in the nineteenth century. Given that the upper windows also date to this final period, it seems likely that the tower was originally raised in height without there ever having been any intention of inserting a second, upper, floor.

The doorway and lower steps of the stair leading up to the roof may be of an earlier date or may, like the rest of the stairway, be the result of nineteenth-century restoration. The battlements with the projecting stone drains below them, whilst being attractive are, nevertheless, fanciful and do not reproduce the medieval arrangements.

A true appreciation of the strategic siting of the castle can be gained from the roof level. From here, you can also see a tree-covered rock knoll in the valley bottom, the site of the earlier, twelfth-century castle.

Returning to courtyard level, notice a short length of curving wall of reddish burnt stone, on a raised area in the corner between the keep and the curtain wall. This is all that remains of a circular oven, and perhaps marks the site of the castle's kitchens. The

Above: The first-floor chamber within the keep. The fireplace is medieval in origin but was restored in the nineteenth century at the same time that the upper window was inserted. A doorway has been inserted into the window embrasure, to the left of the fireplace, which gives access to a stair leading to the roof.

The scant remains of an oven are located in a raised area to the south of the keep, marked by a curving wall of reddish burnt stone.

The west tower was an addition to the original castle design and would have provided extra accommodation that would have been more comfortable and private than that available in the keep. A ground-floor doorway survives on the courtyard side and the remains of a fine fireplace on the first floor.

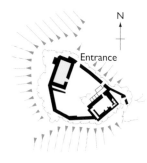

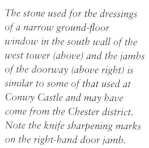

The stone used for the dressings of a narrow ground-floor window in the south wall of the west tower (above) and the jambs of the doorway (above right) is similar to some of that used at Conwy Castle and may have come from the Chester district. Note the knife sharpening marks on the right-hand door jamb.

Right: The remains of the double latrine chamber in the north-east corner of the west tower, which may have served an earlier building on this site.

curtain, standing to between almost 12 and 13 feet (3.7 and 4m), is at its highest along this stretch and varies in thickness between 5 and almost 6 feet (1.5 and 1.8m). Following the curtain wall around to the north you come to a jamb in the wall, which is all that survives of a former opening, possibly an arrowslit.

West Tower

The west tower is clearly a later addition with its south and east walls having been built against the curtain. This may be the *camera* that was under construction in 1283 and would have provided more private and comfortable accommodation than that available in the keep.

It is entered at ground-floor level through a large doorway where only the lower stones of the door jambs survive. These, and the dressings of a narrow ground-floor window in the south wall, are made of a hard white or red-stained sandstone. This is not a local stone. It seems to be similar to some of that used at Conwy Castle and may have come from the Chester district. Knife or arrow-sharpening scratches can be seen in one of the two surviving stones in the right-hand jamb of the doorway. In addition to the window in the south wall, the ground floor was lit by another narrow slit window facing into the courtyard.

A doorway in the north-east corner of the room leads to a chamber with a double latrine. As this is integral with the curtain wall, it must have been built before the tower and may be associated with an earlier building. A separate latrine projection, with two latrines at first-floor level, was added to the curtain at the north-western corner and was presumably contemporary with the construction of the tower.

A fine first-floor fireplace in the east wall has, unfortunately, lost its stone dressings. The only surviving window at this level, located just above the entrance, had a flight of steps leading from its south side up to roof level. No evidence survives of any stairs extending up from ground to first-floor level, suggesting that there may have been internal timber stairs. At a later date, an external stone staircase was added against the south wall of the tower to provide access to the curtain.

A Bird's-Eye View of Dolwyddelan Castle

From the North-East

1 Entrance — Now approached by a modern causeway, the ditch was probably originally spanned by a timber bridge leading to a plain entrance through the curtain wall (p. 25).

2 Ditches — This and the opposite side of the castle were protected by rock-cut ditches with low outer banks (p. 25).

3 Postern Doorway — This led out of the castle from a small additional enclosure only accessible by ladder, or perhaps stairs, leading down from the curtain wall (p. 25).

4 The Keep — Built as a two-storey structure by Llywelyn ab Iorwerth sometime between 1210 and 1240. The tower was heightened, probably by Edward I in the later thirteenth century. It was restored by Lord Willoughby de Eresby in 1848–50 (pp. 11, 18, 25–28).

5 Curtain Wall — Standing to between 12 and 13 feet (3.7 and 4m) high, the curtain wall is at its highest along this stretch. It varies between 5 and almost 6 feet (1.5 and 1.8m) in thickness (p. 28).

6 West Tower — Probably built as the new *camera* by Edward I, it is likely to have replaced an earlier building on the site and provided more spacious accommodation (pp. 17, 28).

7 Latrines — Built into the curtain wall the double latrine chamber may have served an earlier building as well as the west tower (p. 28).

8 Medieval Road — The original road passed the castle on the higher ground to the north-west, not in the valley as it does today (p. 25).

(Illustration by John Banbury)

A Tour of Dolbadarn Castle

Once through the kissing gate immediately below the site, turn to your right and approach the castle from the south-west. At this point, part of the encircling curtain, perhaps containing the original gateway, has been lost. The curtain, like the courtyard buildings, is drystone built and represents the earliest phase of Llywelyn ab Iorwerth's castle. Directly ahead of you, on the highest point of the ridge, stands Llywelyn's imposing round tower, built probably sometime around 1230. Its well-built mortared masonry stands in complete contrast to the drystone footings seen elsewhere. Although the castle was occupied following Edward I's victory in 1283, only the east building seems to date from this period (pp. 20, 34).

The main stone of the castle consists of fair-sized blocks of purple and green slate, but blocks of grit and fine-grained rocks are interspersed in the masonry.

From the rocky outcrop at the far end of the courtyard, away from the round tower, you can appreciate the superb strategic siting of Dolbadarn on a spur between Llyn Padarn and Llyn Peris, guarding the main routeway leading up to the Llanberis Pass and into the heartland of Snowdonia.

The Keep

The keep at Dolbadarn is a very fine example of a Welsh round tower. Well built, it consists of two floors above a basement, unlike most other Welsh towers that date from this time. Clearly, Llywelyn was keen not only to provide comfortable and secure accommodation but also to demonstrate that he could command the resources and skills to build on this scale.

Exterior

Despite the loss of its battlements, the round tower still stands to a height of 46 feet (14m) with a splayed, or battered, base. The main approach is on

the north side up a flight of stone steps leading to a doorway at first-floor level. The doorway was once possibly covered by a porch. The present steps are secondary, but they probably replaced an original timber staircase during the medieval period since the stone steps appear in eighteenth- and nineteenth-century illustrations of the tower as a ruin.

In the face of the tower, to the right of the first-floor doorway and above the steps, you can see five narrow windows. These are all at different levels and light the stairs to the upper storeys and the topmost landing. On the left (north-east) side of the tower is a pent-roofed projection, which contains latrines at first- and second-floor levels. The two outfall chutes can be seen on the outer face near ground level.

The arch over the entrance was restored when the castle was repaired in the late 1940s and early 1950s. The doorway also appears to have undergone some alteration but the original arrangement incorporated a portcullis. For access, this could be drawn up through a slot overhead, to rest in the

Above: Llyn Padarn, looking towards Dolbadarn Castle. The castle is built on a rocky spur and guards the major routeway from the coast, through the Llanberis Pass, into the mountains of Snowdonia.

Opposite: Llywelyn ab Iorwerth's round tower at Dolbadarn remains a remarkable testimony to his power and status.

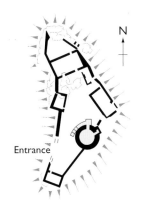

A cutaway reconstruction of the round tower at Dolbadarn as it may have appeared around 1230–40. It is shown with a timber staircase, which was later replaced in stone, and an unusual portcullis arrangement protecting the entrance (Illustration by Chris Jones-Jenkins 1994).

Right: The interior of the keep: the large square holes mark the joists of the timber floors and the crease around the upper level indicates the position of the roof.

Below: This view looks up into the corbelled head of the rectangular projection that housed latrines on the first and second floors of the keep.

window recess on the floor above. Behind the position of the portcullis, the dressed stone sides of the doorway have been robbed away, but a hole for the drawbar, which would have secured the wooden doors, can be seen on the right.

Interior

Entering the tower, you now find yourself on a modern wooden platform. At a slightly lower level you can see the holes that originally housed the floor joists. Beneath these, around the northern side of the tower to your left, there is an offset which provided additional support for the floor. The basement would have been reached by a ladder from a trapdoor in the floor. The only opening into the basement consists of a narrow ventilation shaft sloping upwards to the outer face of the tower. This can be seen at the same level as the floor joists, just below and to the right of the first-floor entrance to the latrines. The purpose of the penannular-shaped structure in the centre of the basement floor remains a mystery.

The doorway to the left of the first-floor entrance, in the northern side of the tower, leads to a latrine lit by a small window. Further around, on the south-east side, there is a narrow window with recessed window seats on either side. The fireplace, which has lost its hood and jambs, has a flue that rises through the thickness of the wall to emerge via a slit in its outer face.

Having almost completed the circuit of the tower at first-floor level, you come to a doorway leading to stairs which wind upwards in an anticlockwise direction, lit by small lights. This brings you to the doorway that led into the principal apartment of the tower, occupying the upper floor. The room has four windows — three with window seats and the fourth with the slot for the portcullis that protected the doorway below — and a well-appointed fireplace with a flue extending up to wall-walk level. From the east window, to the right of the fireplace, a vaulted passage leads down steps to the upper latrine chamber. It was perhaps in this comfortable chamber that Owain Goch dwelt during his imprisonment at Dolbadarn (p. 14).

The main stair, having reversed its spiral, extends upwards to a landing at roof level, before continuing up to the wall-walk. A distinct groove all around the interior of the tower marks the position of the roof, which was protected by the parapet and its long-vanished battlements.

The Courtyard

The curtain wall and all the structures in the courtyard were originally built of drystone masonry although, in places, mortar has been used discreetly during modern consolidation work. Most of the angles of the buildings and curtain wall are bonded, although there are a few butt joints indicating that the buildings of the courtyard are of more than one period.

The curtain wall follows the natural boundary of the ridge except on the south-east, where it was set back from the break of slope when the keep was built. Although now reduced to, at most, just 2 to 3 feet (0.6 to 0.9m) above the level of the courtyard, the curtain probably stood to an original

height of between 10 and 15 feet (3 and 4.5m). Externally, it would have appeared higher in places, particularly at the north-western end, where it extended down to face the outcropping rock. All along the western side and around the northern end of the castle, the curtain has a slight external batter to provide added support for the lower part of the wall.

West Tower

'Tower' is perhaps a misnomer for this rectangular drystone structure, since it could never have stood to any great height. Nevertheless, along with the south tower, it guarded the side of the castle that was most vulnerable to attack, the remainder of the circuit having the defensive benefit of naturally precipitous slopes.

A general view across the courtyard buildings looking north towards Llyn Padarn.

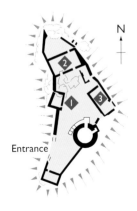

The foundations of the large rectangular building, which extends the full width of the northern end of the courtyard, mark the site of the hall. Note the opposing doorways to the right of the north and south walls that mark the position of a cross-passage.

Hall

At the northern end of the castle is the hall, which stretches across the full width of the courtyard, with doors opposite one another marking the position of a cross-passage. Just beyond the northern doorway of the hall, and immediately to the right, two short walls extending from the outer face of the curtain are all that survive of a latrine. The northern end of the platform terminates in a natural rock boss.

Returning by the way you came, a short length of foundation to the south of the hall marks the position of a small building which was constructed against the eastern curtain. This must have gone out of use before an entrance to the courtyard was inserted into this length of curtain wall, which impinged upon the area of the building and perhaps replaced an earlier entrance to the south.

East Building

The east building is clearly a later addition, breaking through the eastern corner of the courtyard. Although its function is not known, it probably dates from the English occupation of the castle when Dolbadarn had become the centre of a royal manor (p. 20).

Two-thirds of the north-eastern wall of the building is formed by the earlier curtain wall. The stub of masonry at the southern end of this may mark the corner of the original courtyard. The end of this stub,

where it extends into the building, may have formed one side of an entrance through the curtain. This was reached by an exterior flight of steps, the remains of which can still be seen outside the south-east corner of the east building. The remainder of this stretch of the south-east curtain wall must have been removed when the east building was constructed.

The building of the keep led to a reconstruction of the rest of the south-east curtain wall and stretches of this can be seen butting up to the rock outcrop on the north-east side of the keep and extending from its southern side along to the south tower.

Before leaving, it is worth examining the small rectangular south tower which is placed at a point nearest to the road guarding the south-western approach to the castle.

Above: A prince's steward from the Welsh law book of Hywel Dda. His two-coloured gown may indicate the family that he served (National Library of Wales, Peniarth Ms. 28, f. 3v).

Right: The remains of the east building, which was added to the castle at a later date and built partially against the original curtain wall.

A Bird's-Eye View of Dolbadarn Castle

From the North-West

1 Site of Entrance — Although no trace of the original entrance survives, it may have been through this missing section of the curtain wall (p. 31).

2 The Keep — This sophisticated tower was built by Llywelyn ab Iorwerth, probably during the 1230s. It is believed to have been here that Llywelyn ap Gruffudd imprisoned his brother Owain Goch from 1255 until 1277: 'a man who is in the tower, long a guest' (pp. 11–12, 14–15, 31–32).

3 Curtain Wall — Built of drystone masonry, and now reduced to at most 2 to 3 feet (0.6 to 0.9m), it originally stood to between 10 and 15 feet (3 and 4.5m) in height (p. 33).

4 West Tower — Guarding the most vulnerable side of the castle, this rectangular drystone structure could never have stood to any great height (p. 33).

5 Hall — This stretches across the full width of the courtyard. Doors opposite one another mark the position of a cross-passage (p. 34).

6 East Building — Probably added in the late thirteenth century, this building cuts across the line of the curtain wall (p. 34).

7 South Tower — A drystone structure placed at a point nearest to the road guarding the south-western approach to the castle (p. 34).

8 Llyn Peris — The castle was strategically sited on a spur between Llyn Peris and Llyn Padarn, guarding the main routeway leading up to the Llanberis Pass (p. 31).

(Illustration by John Banbury)

A Tour of Castell y Bere

Today, the ruinous masonry stretching along the summit of a rocky outcrop on the eastern side of the Dysynni valley is generally accepted as being the remains of the castle that Llywelyn ab Iorwerth established in 1221, after he took possession of the *cantref* of Meirionnydd and the adjoining commote of Ardudwy (p. 8). The picturesque and remote location makes it difficult to appreciate that this sprawling stronghold once controlled an important routeway running up from the coast at Tywyn northwards through the mountains towards Dolgellau and protected the southern border of Gwynedd. Moreover, such was the significance of this castle to Edward I that in 1283 he gave express orders for its security and later established a free borough here (p. 19).

Nevertheless, much of what remains dates from the time of Llywelyn ab Iorwerth, although the south tower could equally be the work of his grandson, Llywelyn ap Gruffudd, and the thick curtain walls that enclose the ditch yard almost certainly date from the English occupation (p. 19).

Before beginning your tour, note that the outcrop upon which the castle stands has strong natural defences to the north and west. The builders supplemented these with rock-cut ditches on the remaining sides, although that at the north-east end is very slight and may be no more than a quarry. Taking the path from the small car park towards the entrance at a second kissing gate, you cross a flat area that is one possible site of the borough (p. 19). Once through the gate, immediately on your right, you will see a stretch of rock-cut ditch with the remains of the eastern curtain wall on the summit above. Follow the path to the southern end of the castle where, rounding the perimeter, you will see another defensive ditch on the right, cutting the castle off from the south-western end of the ridge.

The Gateway and Courtyard

The medieval approach to the castle from the valley bottom would have been up the long slope from the south-west, just to your left. This meets the present path near the outer of three ditches protecting the main gateway, the south-eastern end of which has been filled in to take the path.

The second ditch is now spanned by a modern bridge. Beneath the inner end of this bridge, you will see the foundations of the outermost of two gate-towers, which still contains its drawbridge pit. The outer walls of the barbican run away to either side; that on the less vulnerable west side is considerably thinner than its eastern counterpart. As you climb the stone steps, note the various wall foundations on each side. Today it is difficult to recreate the form of the original buildings, which may date from different periods in the castle's development, especially given their advanced design (p. 9). However, the large building to the right of the steps may have been some form of guardroom.

The upper bridge crosses the third, narrow, ditch towards the inner gate. This gate is one of the few places in the castle to have retained any dressed masonry. On either side, beneath the bridge, the large recesses in the stonework would have originally housed the pivot of another drawbridge. Just beyond this point, grooves on either side of the passage may have housed a portcullis, although they may have been too wide to have served this function. Gates were hung behind the door jambs, the bases of which survive on either side of the passage. A slot for the hinge of one of the gates is still visible just beyond the right-hand jamb.

Passing through the gateway, you enter the main courtyard of the castle. The inconvenient position of the castle well or cistern, immediately in front of you, was probably determined by the geology of the

The elaborate entrance arrangements to Castell y Bere, with the round tower astride the curtain in the background.

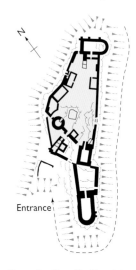

Entrance

Opposite: Castell y Bere is perched on a remote rocky outcrop in the Dysynni valley, close to the lower slopes of Cadair Idris. The origin of its name is not known for certain though it has been traced to 'bera' meaning bird of prey and 'bere' meaning 'the shank or spur of the hill': given its location, both names are equally applicable.

Above: A wooden bucket restored from fragments of oak found in the well (National Museum of Wales).

Top right: The courtyard, looking north from the middle tower. The well or cistern is in the foreground.

Middle right: The postern in the curtain wall adjacent to the round tower. The change in stonework around the door indicates that it must have been a later insertion.

Bottom right: The apsidal or elongated D-shaped north tower. The thick screen walls seen in the foreground of this view protected the ground-floor entrance.

Entrance

castle rock. Indeed, the overall irregular topography of the site is a characteristic found in other Welsh castles and access must have always been on horseback or by foot.

To the left, the round tower, with its basal batter, sits astride the west curtain wall. Like all the other towers in the castle it originally consisted of two storeys. Steps led up to a raised sill and then down into the basement while access to the upper floor could have been by either an external wooden stair, a ladder from the basement, or directly from the curtain wall. Just beyond the tower, a postern doorway in the corner of the courtyard led out into the barbican. Drawbar holes survive either side of the doorway. Viewed from outside, a change from the flat stones around the doorway to the more irregular masonry seen elsewhere in the surrounding wall shows that the doorway must be a later insertion.

Two rectangular buildings of unknown date occupy the north-western side of the courtyard. Between the furthest, northernmost, building and the west curtain wall there is an external flight of stairs at the end of a short passage, which suggests that both buildings were two storeys high. A doorway at the foot of the stairs led to a latrine block projecting out from the curtain, which would have served both ground- and first-floor levels.

The footings of another rectangular building survive on the opposite side of the courtyard. Originally, the whole inner area would have been filled with ranges of buildings and associated structures that would have served the domestic needs of the castle, including kitchens, stables and stores, although today it is impossible to determine the original function of any of these. A second postern doorway can be seen in the northern corner of the courtyard. Given the precipitous nature of the ground outside, this was probably only intended for use in times of emergency.

The North Tower

The north tower, at the far end of the courtyard, adopts the characteristically Welsh apsidal or elongated D-shaped plan. It was entered at both ground- and first-floor level. The stone stair

to the first floor is of two periods, and may have had a timber predecessor. The original ground-floor doorway was subsequently protected by a thick screen wall, which appears to have been contemporary with the second stair, and would have provided both a ground- and first-floor extension to the west side of the tower. The discovery of finely-dressed stonework in the rubble of this tower has led to the suggestion that there may have been a chapel at first-floor level. However, comparison with similar structures elsewhere, at Dolforwyn Castle and Dryslwyn Castle for example, suggests that the pillar in the middle of the ground floor would have supported a hearth on the floor above. This would suggest that the first-floor chamber served as a hall rather than a chapel. Nevertheless, a small chapel in the south-east-facing apsidal end of the tower should not be ruled out.

Beyond the north tower there is a further defensive ditch protecting the northern end of the ridge (not accessible). As you leave the north tower, on your left is the best surviving stretch of curtain wall, with steps that led up to the wall-walk.

The Middle Tower

The middle tower, like the rest of the castle's towers, was of two storeys. It is situated at the highest point on the castle rock and probably served as the original keep. The present entrance to the unlit ground-floor room appears to have been forced through the masonry at a later date, probably at the same time as the external stone stair to the upper floor was added, perhaps replacing an earlier timber stair.

The enclosed area beyond the middle tower is known as the ditch yard. Unlike today, where there are modern breaches through the walls at each end of the platform alongside the middle tower, the ditch yard was originally only accessible via the wall-walk from which a stair would presumably have led to ground level. From the modern bridge over the substantial rock-cut ditch, you can see a postern doorway in the curtain wall at the south-eastern end of the ditch.

Originally, the middle tower may have formed the southern extremity of the castle, before the south tower was added. The thick walls of the ditch yard were built later to secure the area between the two towers (p. 8).

Entrance

Below: The ditch yard looking towards the south tower.

Left: The middle tower is the best preserved building at Castell y Bere and, like the other towers, would have stood two storeys high. Both stairs appear to be later additions, perhaps inserted at the same time that the ground-floor door was knocked through the thick masonry walls. The tower probably served as the original keep and would have been entered at first-floor level, perhaps via a timber staircase.

The southern apsidal tower (above) may have been a later addition to the castle by Llywelyn ap Gruffudd. The spacious ground-floor room contains three embrasures, which narrowed to arrowslits, and was served by a latrine chamber (right) accessed from a passage in the thickness of the wall.

The South Tower

The massive south-west wall of the ditch yard was built directly against the rear wall of the D-shaped, or apsidal, south tower. An extended entrance passage leads to the ground-floor doorway into the tower. On the right, a further doorway opens to a flight of stairs that was originally lit by a small slit, which was blocked when the ditch yard wall was built. This stair led to the upper floor

of the tower and subsequently gave access to the ditch yard wall-walk.

The ground floor comprised a spacious room containing three wide embrasures, originally narrowing to arrowslits. On the left, the doorway halfway along the length of the room led into a passage running southwards in the thickness of the wall to a latrine chamber that served the rooms at both floor levels. There is no evidence of a fireplace at this level and the main apartment would have been on the first floor, possibly with a central hearth as in the north tower.

Entrance

Further Reading

R. Avent, *Cestyll Tywysogion Gwynedd — Castles of the Princes of Gwynedd* (Cardiff 1983).

R. Avent, *Criccieth Castle* (Cadw, Cardiff 1989).

R. Avent, 'Castles of the Welsh Princes', *Château Gaillard* **16** (1994), 11–20.

L. A. S. Butler, 'Medieval Finds from Castell-y-Bere, Merioneth', *Archaeologia Cambrensis* **123** (1974), 78–112.

L. A. S. Butler and J. K. Knight, *Dolforwyn Castle — Montgomery Castle* (Cadw, Cardiff, 2004).

L. A. S. Butler, 'The Castles of the Princes of Gwynedd' in D. M. Williams and J. R. Kenyon, editors, *The Impact of the Edwardian Castles in Wales* (Oxford 2010).

A. D. Carr and G. Carr, *Cestyll Gwynedd* (Cadw, Cardiff 1985).

R. R. Davies, *Conquest, Coexistence, and Change: Wales 1063–1415* (Oxford 1987); reprinted in paperback as, *The Age of Conquest: Wales 1063–1415* (Oxford 1991).

E. D. Evans, 'Castell y Bere', *Journal of the Merioneth Historical and Record Society* **3** (1957–60), 31–44.

G. R. J. Jones, 'The Defences of Gwynedd in the Thirteenth Century', *Transactions of the Caernarvonshire Historical Society* **30** (1969), 29–43.

P. Joyner, editor, *Dolbadarn: Studies on a Theme* (Aberystwyth 1990).

C. A. R. Radford, *Dolbadarn Castle* (HMSO, London 1948)

C. A. R. Radford, *Dolwyddelan Castle* (HMSO, London 1946).

Royal Commission on Ancient and Historical Monuments in Wales and Monmouthshire, *Inventory of Ancient Monuments in Caernarvonshire*, I, East (London 1956), 80–82; II, Central (London 1960), 165–68.

D. Renn and R. Avent *Flint Castle — Ewloe Castle*, second edition (Cadw, Cardiff 2001).

J. B. Smith, *Llywelyn ap Gruffudd* (Cardiff 1998).

J. B. Smith & Ll. B. Smith, editors, *History of Merioneth, II, The Middle Ages* (Cardiff 2001), 50–55, 386–421.

D. Stephenson, *The Governance of Gwynedd* (Cardiff 1984).

A. Taylor, *The Welsh Castles of Edward I* (London 1986).

R. Turvey, *The Welsh Princes 1063–1283* (Harlow 2002).

R. Turvey, *Llywelyn the Great* (Llandysul 2007).

J. Wynn (edited by J. G. Jones), *The History of the Gwydir Family and Memoirs* (Llandysul 1990).